LUIS ZAFRA ZAFRA

Personal Growth for
Professional Development

THE BENEFITS OF STORYTELLING AND THE PERSONAL NARRATIVE FOR YOUR WORK LIFE

6 secrets to build your Personal Brand based on credibility and trust.

#IMPROVFORLIFE

Executive production LNG LLC
Literary editor Viviana Andrea Fontecha Donoso
Graphic Design and Editing Carlos Felipe González

I would have to thank a lot of people for this first editorial step in my life, but naming them all would be a long task and I might leave someone out and I wouldn't like that; therefore, I want to thank someone for whom I feel special gratitude since he is the one who makes things happen forcefully in my life for the last few years, my friend "mi Lanza".

Hello!

My name is Luis and I'm very happy that you have this book in your hands today.

A few years back, I discovered the impact that a good story can have on people. At first, I believed that Storytelling could only be used to entertain people with my anecdotes. Then I began to realize that *knowing how to tell people* my story helped me in my work.

Have you ever thought that, regardless of whether you are an employee, independent, industry manager, entrepreneur, boss or subordinate, you are the product? - the person who provides the service experience of YOUR PERSONAL BRAND?

The basic principle of your reality demands you to become aware of two things:

- ✓ Be conscious of who you are and how you project yourself to others.

- ✓ That is to say, to be coherent between what you think, feel, say and perform.

Storytelling and Personal Narrative is the conscious way of telling who you are through the coherence of what you express — both verbally and through your body language — in order to build relationships based on credibility and trust.

Your Personal Brand is the reconciliation between the essence of who you are and how that is reflected in what you do.

The question then is:

How do you want to be remembered?

Today I want to tell you how you can use Storytelling and Personal Narrative in job interviews, presentations, meetings with your managers and/or subordinates ... to be remembered the right way for the right reasons.

Luis Zafra Zafra

WHAT IS STORYTELLING AND PERSONAL NARRATIVE?

Storytelling is the art of telling a story, but not just any story told in any way. It is not just about narrating an event or an experience.

It is about telling a story in such a way that you connect with your audience, so that you engage their thinking, reflection, and emotion. Those are the stories that will be remembered.

Why?

Because a story that makes you feel will make you think. And that is the way to incite actions that change behaviors.

And what about personal narrative?

As the name implies, it's the art of telling your personal story.

Now, when Storytelling and Personal Narrative come together, something *magical* happens.

You learn to narrate who you are and what you are capable of accomplishing from your personal story.

That is, you build your Personal Brand expressing what you know, what you feel and the experience developed from what you've lived through in the roles and environments of your daily life.

Storytelling and Personal Narrative not only tells an anecdote or provides a message, but it **traces a path** that leaves a mark of who you are in others.

And how do you do it if you've never done it?

The most obvious answer is by practicing.

However, I understand the fear of facing a new experience. For that reason, I wrote this book to serve as your personal roadmap every time you want to express yourself through your stories and, thus, build a Personal Brand based on credibility and trust.

1

SECRET: DEFINE YOUR GOALS

When you tell your anecdotes and stories, are you clear about the message you want to deliver?

Remember that you are building your **Personal Brand**. That is why it is important that you are clear about the image you want to project when telling your story.

There is nothing worse than wanting to impress your boss or co-workers with a story that makes you look like a clown, a tyrant or even worse, an incompetent individual.

Storytelling and Personal Narrative helps you build and tell your stories through the definition of **three fundamental objectives:**

Why?

It's the clarity and the logic when selecting your story.
Why do you choose that story and not a different one?

What For?

It's the purpose you have in telling that story.
What is the message or impression you
want to leave once the narrative is over?

Higher search

It's a statement - the objective that contains the 2
previous questions. It has to do with the clarity of the
expression of your Personal Brand from 2 aspects:

-How is it that you want to be remembered? Where is
it that you want to take your personal image?

- The way you want others to observe you, what is it
you want to tell and leave about yourself in each of
those stories?

LUIS ZAFRA ZAFRA
Personal Growth for
Professional Development

IT'S TIME FOR YOUR TRAINING

All the time you are revealing yourself. You continually tell others who you are, how you are, and what you seek through the way you establish your relationships and convey — in each of your environments and roles — what you have to say.

It is therefore very important that you work on a conscious narrative exercise, beginning with defining the sequence of your objectives. From these simple exercises, you will be able to generate awareness of what you say and how you say it.

1. Why?

This observation must be made in two tenses:

- **In the Past** ... remembering.
- **In the Present** ... listening to yourself.

a. Remember and identify what themes are most often present in your life.

b. Review what the stories of your life and the anecdotes are, whether your own or borrowed, that you use the most to talk about yourself, to tell what you like or what you value.

Write here what you want to clarify:

- **Why** you like these topics:

____
____
____
____.

- **How** you identify with them:

____
____
____
____.

- **Why** that story proves it for you:

____
____
____
____.

2. What for?

You always do what you do because you have something in mind (the interest) ... whether conscious or not, you want to obtain some result. Just think that when you are planning to win someone's affection, your way of communicating and revealing yourself seeks to position yourself as an attractive being in front of the other person. When you are in front of an audience, you seek to seduce them and show yourself to them as someone reliable, knowledgeable or an expert in a subject. That is to say, credible.

But this exercise is not always done consciously; rather, it responds to sociocultural impulses that sometimes seem to be involuntary. It is as if you should be and behave in one way or another, because of the presumed "role" you play.

Therefore, it is important to raise, as much as you can, your level of awareness about **the goal you seek when choosing and using one or another story or anecdote.** This will help your narratives adhere less and less to stereotypes and more to who you are.

The question here is:

Do you really know what goal you want to achieve when you choose a story or a way to tell it?

In the last 2 weeks and taking into account the various roles of your life at work, with your partner, with your children, public speaking, etc., answer the following questions:

- How aware have you been of the goals you are looking for when communicating about yourself?

____
____
____
____
____.

- How conscious have you been about the way you've chosen to tell about yourself?

____

____

____

____

____.

- Do you perceive a difference between the times you have consciously told about yourself and those you have not?

____

____

____

____

____.

3. Higher search.

You might want many things and you might be a dreamer; however, it is also very likely that you do not have much clarity regarding the image of that dream and how you will achieve it. (Does it sound familiar?)

The invitation is that you dare to imagine but, above all, to formally manifest who you want to be and think about how to achieve it.

To do this, answer these questions:

- How do you want to be remembered by others? (Try to be detailed in the description of what you want, identifying the mark you want to leave on others.)

____
____
____
____.

- How do you want others to observe you? (That is, how do you want to leave that mark, doing what and getting what results in your life?)

____
____
____
____.

These last two questions will surely inspire the need to think of an action plan to achieve what you want. Don't lose sight of that. It can be the beginning of structuring a life project. It's all up to you.

4. Choose one of the stories you use most to talk about yourself identified in exercise 1. Then apply each of the 3 exercises to that particular story.

2 SECRET: KEEP IN MIND THE ELEMENTS OF A GOOD STORY

Do you know how to tell stories in a logical sequence? Or are you one of those who opens "parentheses" to clarify something you already said?

If your story does not have order and a logical sequence, you will hardly reach the 3 objectives you have set.

Therefore, you will not project the image you want and expect.

So if you don't want this to happen to you, it is important that you are clear about the elements that are part of your story and that will help you build a **credible and reliable Personal Brand.**

Message

Determine in advance, what is the message you want to leave when telling your story.

Characters / Context

Choose the characters that intervene in your narrative and the place where the events take place.

Plot

Organize the set of events that happen throughout your story that support or exemplify the message you chose.

Conflict

Present the particular obstacle or problem that your characters face that will allow you to reveal your message.

Outcome

Resolve the conflict giving meaning to the message you want to deliver.

IT'S TIME FOR YOUR TRAINING

All the stories you tell have these elements, some better worked than in others. Or, sometimes, they can be so clearly ignored that you identify their absence. Knowing their existence and importance allows you to work decisively to take advantage of them, either technically or intuitively.

Choose one of the stories in your life that you like to tell the most or an anecdote that is meaningful to you. (You can refer to exercise 1 of the previous chapter). After defining your 3 goals, concentrate on identifying each of the 5 parts of your story. Write each of them in the following template, so you can see how you're using them:

Element	Description	Feedback
Message		
Character/Context		
Plot		
Conflict		
Outcome		

Once you've placed the pieces of your story on the template, find an opportunity where you can tell your story to someone you know. At the end of your story, ask him or her: How did you perceive each of the parts of my story? Write down the answers. This feedback will help you identify what connects with the audience and the unnecessary information that does not allow understanding of your message with the clarity you expect.

3 SECRET: IT'S BETTER *TO BE* THAN TO *APPEAR TO BE*

Currently, there is an eagerness to present yourself in a way to gain value by feeling envied or admired by your social network.
This eagerness can make you fall for the lie that it is more important to be perceived than to actually be what you reveal.

Your personal construction and growth will always be more important than an arrogant image. Personal Branding isn't just the packaging — the way others see you — it's everything you are and leave in your relationship with others.

Therefore, it is essential that you begin to be aware of who you are today, with your positive characteristics and opportunities for improvement. Identify how you would like to be seen and admired so you can draw up a plan of action to get where you want to go in a consistent manner.

The important thing will always be

to be as you seem.

IT'S TIME FOR YOUR TRAINING

One of the most important adventures in life is knowing yourself. That possibility of being aware of who you are and what you **do** have.

However, it is not always easy to access that self-knowledge because we have been taught to see ourselves in two ways: one, underestimating our abilities and qualities; the other is overestimating them.

Without a doubt, that hurts us. The right way is to see and value ourselves in a balanced way, in such a way that allows us to enjoy ourselves while we are clear about the wide growth potential that each person has.

So be prepared to give yourself a moment with yourself, one that can reveal your qualities, your possibilities for improvement and, especially, the possibility of seeking your own balanced view of yourself.

Fill out the following table, as honestly as you can:

-On the left column write the 5 best qualities that you possess - those that make you who you are.

-On the right column write the 5 possibilities for improvement - those things that you know will make you a better person if you change them.

Each of the qualities and opportunities for improvement should be described in detail.

Note: There must be 5 of each, no more, no less.

Qualities	Opportunities for improvement.

Once you've finished filling out the table, answer the following questions:

After seeing yourself from this perspective, how do you feel you value yourself? Do you underestimate, overestimate or feel balanced on your self-observation?

____

____

____

____

____

____.

Sometimes we are so eager to be heard, to say what we have to tell or to be seen as we want to be seen, that we forget that human reality is relational.

If only one of the parties has the opportunity, the time and space to express himself/herself, the others will begin to lose interest.

This means that you need to establish relationships with other people, characterized by the quality of the two-way bond between the parties.

One of the basic steps for Storytelling and Personal Storytelling is <u>listening</u>.

Yes, **listen to understand** the context you are in and the people who are in it. Thus, you will be able to perceive what happens and the way people relate, to better choose the part of you that you reveal and the way you do it.

IT'S TIME FOR YOUR TRAINING

You can do some exercises in your everyday life that will allow you to train your ability to listen. Once you've done that, write down in detail how you felt and what effects it had on the situation.

1. Do not interrupt while the other person is talking.
If you want to step in and give your opinion, wait for the other person to finish talking...

How did you feel doing this?

____
____
____
____
____
____.

What effects did that action have on the situation?

____
____
____
____
____
____.

2. **Avoid constructing your arguments while the other person is talking.** When you start building your case while the other person is talking, **you're not listening** or **present.** Listen and take a few seconds to think about your answer and how you're going to say it.

How did you feel doing this?

____
____
____
_____________________________________.

What effects did that action have on the situation?

____
____
____
_____________________________________.

3. **Stop assuming.** Don't assume you know in advance what the other person is going to say and the motivations behind his/her words. **Take the time to listen.**

How did you feel doing this?

____
____
____
_____________________________________.

What effects did that action have on the situation?

____
____
____
_____________________________________.

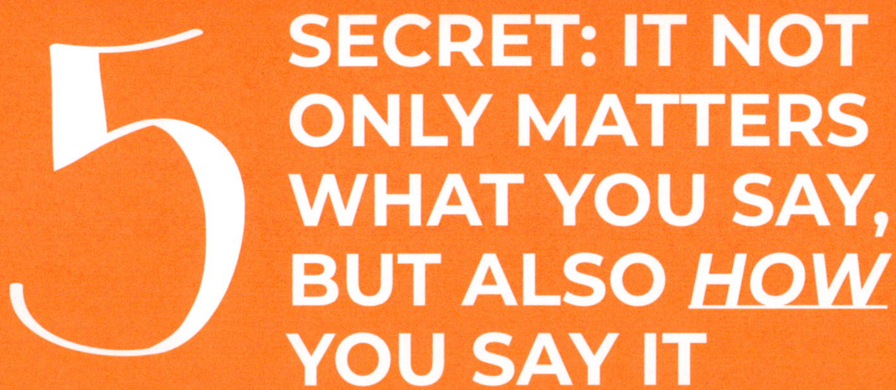

"Having a well-crafted speech is the important thing."
Will that be the only important thing when it comes to telling you to build your Personal Brand?

While it is true that a well-crafted speech is very valuable when it comes to interacting with people in all areas, it is not the only thing that counts.

Just imagine yourself in a job interview where you think you have the correct and adequate answers. Or in a presentation to a large audience, where you have your ideas clear and everything you have to say flows. That's always a major benefit.

However, you cannot forget – let alone neglect – your body language. Many times it is possible to see the inconsistency between what is being said with words and what is expressed with facial and body gestures.

Speaking fluently and in an organized manner while your face reflects stage fright and your body expresses the desire to run away is definitely **not coherent nor does it build credibility and confidence. Goodbye accurate and proper answers. I will see you soon clarity.**

Understanding yourself as an expressive unit is fundamental when doing the exercise of telling about yourself.

How do you do it?

You train yourself in 3 fundamental aspects:

- ✓ Verbal speech (what to say, content, perfect words, etc.).

- ✓ The gestural expression (without concealing or appearing).

- ✓ Be present and sincerely committed to managing your emotions at all times (avoid the "present body, absent mind" situation).

These 3 elements will help you to be honest with what you express and it will contribute **to avoid the image of a robot fulfilling a programmed task.**

IT'S TIME FOR YOUR TRAINING

One of the most important things when working and growing in the art of Storytelling and Personal Narrative, is that there should be conjunction between what you think you are expressing and what others are receiving and interpreting from you.

Although it is very difficult for this to be perfect, the closer they are the better, and your work will be more effective and productive.

A good part of the inconsistencies that exist in the communication exercise is the de-synchronization and de-tuning of these three concepts:

That's why it's so important to develop **awareness of your personal performance.**

Do the exercise of telling one of your stories or anecdotes in one of your usual environments. Once finished, describe:

How did you feel?

How do you think you were impacting people with the way you told your story?

How much do you remember about interacting with people and their reactions?

Then ask someone (or several people, if you can):

How did they perceive you?

What did they understand about your story?

How did you make them feel?

When you have the answers, you can compare and contrast your feelings with your audience's experience. This exercise will provide you with the necessary information to generate learning and develop actions to improve your ability to tell about yourself through your stories.

YOUR PERCEPTION	YOUR AUDIENCE'S PERCEPTION
How did you feel?	How did they perceive you?
How do you think you were impacting people with the way you told your story?	What did they understand about your story?
How much do you remember about interacting with people and their reactions?	How did you make them feel?

"Everything has to be rehearsed for it to go perfectly."
Could it be that this is how life works?

In my life this was a great conflict because I trained as an actor in a classical school. There the preparation and the work consisted of rehearsing a lot and with careful dedication so that the result at the time of presenting the piece was perfect.

But, at the same time, I trained in Theatrical Improvisation. The world of Improv presents you with the here and now as the total expression of your present existence.

The truth is that life is not of extremes or static.

Life happens in a dynamic balance of permanent adjustments, which allow you to use what you learn assertively and productively.

It is very important to be clear about the path, the structure of what you want to say and how you will do it; but, it is equally important to learn to improvise.

This will allow you to be present, consciously, to relate with people in a real way. This implies that:

> Improvising is the ability to generate as many answers as possible to choose the best option for the situation that arises, without your mind going blank or being *paralyzed* by fear.

✓ Live and manage your emotions and those of your audience.

✓ Make the rational elaborations necessary to live a mutual experience of transformation with your audience.

LUIS ZAFRA ZAFRA
Personal Growth for
Professional Development

IT'S TIME FOR YOUR TRAINING

When it comes to being on stage (or at least being the protagonist of a moment in a meeting, giving a talk or driving a moment in front of an audience — large or not) it's easy to feel fear or stress. Two types of attitudes also tend to arise to take on these challenges:

The first is the path **of control and perfection.** You try to ensure that everything is structured, detailed written and organized, as well as rehearsed so as not to leave details to chance and thus avoid any inconvenience that may surprise you.

While this path is an alternative that seeks tranquility through total control of circumstances, it is important to say that life cannot be controlled. Situations can change or alter what you had prepared, causing it to be partially or totally modified.

The great risk of this path is that it can make you **inflexible and not very adaptive**, generating a lot of pressure and even panic when facing unanticipated conditions.

The second path is that **of absolute freedom and total freshness.** In this case, you fully trust both your abilities and the possibility of establishing a fresh and real relationship from the unsuspected interaction with the public.

This path brings a dose of adrenaline and extreme experience of the here and now, but its risk lies in the fact that, by not having clearly defined the objectives and depending more on the living relationship with the audience, you can **deviate from what is important.** The above will prevent you from being clear, meaningful and contributing to others, while delivering your message.

As I told you before, how you do it is just as important as what you tell (content). Therefore, choose one of your favorite stories to do the following exercise:

1. Define the sequence of goals: why, what for and align them with your higher search.

2. Clearly organize the table of elements of your story: message, characters and context, plot, conflict and outcome.

3. Think about the path of the story. Foresee a route that leads you towards the established objectives in a fluid and natural way – leaving space for live interaction – but at the same time providing the clarity of a defined and organized passage that gives forcefulness to the narrative.

To build such a route, use the **narrative step outline.**

Take your story to review the content and sequence of events that compose it; that is, each of the moments that you consider important. Give them a name and a descriptive phrase of their content.

Organize them into a list that shows the narrative journey from beginning to end so you can remember in order how your story is going, defining each moment and its importance. This will allow you **to properly manage the time** of each moment and the emphasis you want to give each of them.

I leave you with an example using the story of Little Red Riding Hood.

Little Red Riding Hood Narrative Step Outline.

1. Greet the audience.
2. Introduction of the story "Little Red Riding Hood".
3. Presentation of the characters and context of Little Red Riding Hood and Mom.
4. Announce what is requested of her: Bring some food to her grandmother.
5. Announce the danger involved: The character of the Wolf is introduced.
6. Illustration of the encouraging walk through the forest. In parallel, the stalking of the Wolf is generated.
7. The Wolf approaches Little Red Riding Hood: He tricks her right at the crossroads.
8. Little Red Riding Hood, in her innocence, allows herself to be deceived.
9. Side Events: The Wolf arrives at Grandma's house and devours her while Little Red Riding Hood, exhausted, makes the long way.
10. Little Red Riding Hood arrives at Grandma's house: She finds the door open, which causes her concern. Her suspicion increases when she has the dialogue of questions with the grandmother.
11. Surprise Attack of the Wolf: Little Red Riding Hood ends up being eaten, too, in one bite.
12. The Wolf is more than satisfied: Illustration of a Wolf overwhelmed by fullness, lying on the ground and asleep.
13. Appearance of the hero: The hunter who has chased the Wolf, finds him lying down. Saves Little Red Riding Hood and Grandma.
14. Moment of reinforcement of the message.
15. Thanks and farewell.

It's time to train

Remember that the protagonist of your life IS YOU.

Building a reliable and credible Personal Brand is in your hands.

Train, exercise and plan.

But keep in mind that things don't always go as you expect.

So don't let fear paralyze you.

Improvise!

MEET
#IMPROVFORLIFE

#ImprovForLife is the methodology I designed to help people **fulfill their dreams and enjoy life.** The two main pillars of #ImprovForLife are:

The playfulness in the here and now of Improvisation.

The therapeutic insight of Psychology.

#ImprovForLife is a methodology that helps you in:

Your personal growth. You will learn to take charge of your life, to stop depending on others and circumstances to be who you want to be and live the life you want. You will strengthen your internal structure, while clarifying your meaning and life project.

Your professional development. You will develop competencies that will allow you to perform better at work and to foster healthier relationships. This will make you stand out for the right reasons.

WHAT ARE THE BENEFITS OF TRAINING WITH #IMPROVFORLIFE?

- You're going to have fun as you discover who you are, what **YOUR skills are, and what you want for your life.**

- You will learn by doing. What is valuable is not what you learn **but what you put into practice in your life.**

- The protagonist of your life is YOU. Therefore, for me it is important to help you answer 3 fundamental questions:

  ✓ Who are you?

  ✓ Who do you want to be?

  ✓ How do you want to be remembered?

- **You will gain security and confidence in yourself,** by taking on new personal and work challenges.

- You will learn to lower the levels of stress and conflict in your relationships, since you will be able to:

✓ **Express how you feel without hurting others** (by exploding), or hurting yourself (by remaining silent).

✓ Listen to **communicate and resolve.**

- You will feel how you **take charge** of your life **by empowering** yourself with your abilities and being aware of your abilities.

- You will identify what your **unique value** is that makes you **memorable.**

Train with me, find out who you are and what you are capable of doing.

Learn to properly manage your emotions, improve your communication, and build healthier, more productive relationships.

Enhancing your soft skills with #ImprovForLife will make you an **important and contributing** person in your environment.

LUIS ZAFRA ZAFRA

Personal Growth for Professional Development

www.luiszafra.com

 Luis@luiszafra.com

 @lfzafra

 Luis Zafra Zafra

 Luis Zafra

Made in the USA
Monee, IL
07 July 2026

56553668R00024